Everything I Know About
Self-esteem I Got From Gehazi

By Dr. Philip Oldfield

Dedication

I would like to dedicate this book to my Dad, who intuitively and perhaps even without realizing it, encouraged me to take up various indoor activities which helped develop my self-esteem and self-image. Without my dad, I would probably have never got into the sciences in the first place.

Table of Contents

Chapters

1.   Introduction

We all have times when we get mistreated at school, or work, or wherever; resulting in being put down, constantly being criticized, not being able to seemingly do anything right. Well, if that's you, rest assured, you are not alone, it's happened to me as well. Being in such an environment can, potentially, destroy a person. Everyone longs to feel good about themselves, and so they should.   I wish that everyone could feel good about themselves. The problem is that when people are being put down continuously it results in low self-esteem which can lead to rebellious attitudes and bad choices.

We are going to go back in time to the year 850 BC. This story is about a man who, if we are honest; most of us should relate to. Nearly everyone I spoke to, at least within Christian circles, didn't seem to know who he was until I mentioned whose servant he was. It's strange how certain people seem to skip our memory; but to be fair he's not mentioned much. He starts off well enough, but what happened? The fact of the matter is that we all need to be appreciated, and when that doesn't happen, it's a recipe for trouble.

So in "Everything I know about self-esteem I got from Gehazi" we are going to look at the conditions that contributed to Gehazi's poor decisions and we will try to understand what may have been going through his head at the time.   There are a lot of sermons which equate Gehazi with greed to the extreme. I would like to propose that all he ever wanted was some appreciation and positive recognition, and that for too long he's been getting a bad rap.

Don't believe me? Refer to the maker's manual:

(The Bible, 1 Kings 19:19 to 2 Kings 8:5). Bible verses will be appropriately paraphrased, not quoted. However, Biblical references will be indicated for your information.

2.   About the Author

In my first book "Everything I know About Stress Management I Got From Elijah" I included a general introduction about myself. So that you don't get bored hearing the same thing over again, I'm going to talk about something specific that happened to me when I was young and how my dad helped me develop a good self-image, and self-esteem. In my previous book I mentioned that I was born with a lung condition (bronco pulmonary dysplasia: I was a premature baby, put in an oxygen tent for too long and so my lungs didn't develop properly).

I was chronically ill when I was younger, at the age seven I would get up in the night coughing up blood, over the kitchen sink. The only thing that seemed to help was a nice mug of hot tea, which I would make for myself. On one occasion, I actually found myself cursing a God I did not believe in or even knew existed and wanted to be put out of my misery because I was in such a lot of pain. I then turned round only to see my dad; and as soon as I stared at him, he just burst into tears (I seem to have that effect on people even now). I remember thinking at the time it should be me that's crying not him! What I didn't know at the time was that he blamed himself for my condition (thinking it was genetic), when in fact it was his smoking that gave him his lung trouble. I just stared at him, we didn't say a word to each other, he then left, I had my mug of tea and eventually went to bed.

In the weeks that followed I noticed that he took an interest in what I was doing in my spare time. I was very interested in electronics (I was working on a few projects), and was an avid science fiction fan. My dad then started to bring in radios, televisions, tape recorders, and record players for me to repair. Some of them I could keep for myself. Others, once they were repaired would go back to their owners - his friends from the local pub. They would pay my dad, and I would get a percentage. He would also buy a monthly magazine for me called Practical Electronics, to encourage my interests.

As a treat, he took my brothers and I to see the Dr. Who films at the cinema; and yes there were films! I must have driven my parents crazy shouting out the word "exterminate" like a demented five-year old over and over again, and threatening them with the toilet plunger. No wonder people are terrified of the Daleks, I mean who wants a toilet plunger in the face. I had a lot of fun back then....and I still do!

Looking back on it now, my dad's encouragement did wonders for my self-esteem and helped enormously to develop direction in my life at such an early age.

The key to it all was this - he did not do everything for me, but gave me the support and resources to be successful on my own leading to

positive self-esteem, and the rewards for my efforts was all part and parcel of it.

Before he died I was able to thank him for everything he did for me; it's been over 20 years now.......and I still miss him.

3.   Valley of Vision

That is what Gehazi's name means: "valley of vision" and I think he lived up to his name, at least initially. Very keen, wanted to serve, and we have no idea how he and Elisha first met. He had great expectations of himself where God would lead him, he was highly motivated and there's nothing wrong with that, in and of itself. It is very rare that a person goes into a new job and immediately lacks motivation. What usually happens is that he or she, for one reason or another, loses motivation over a period of time. Sometimes, after a while the person ends up just doing the bare minimum.

You may think to yourself; what has this got to do with me? Well it may be closer than you think; let me tell you what happened to me a few years back. Let's face it, most of us, if not all, have been discouraged at work when doing your best and really working hard and then some else gets promoted! It's not the fault of the person who got promoted, and not once did I ever take it that way, but it was none the less discouraging. So I went up to my boss at that time and asked what would be required to get a promotion; and in return got a whole list of requirements; all of which over a two year period were fulfilled, still no promotion.

In the end he told me in no uncertain terms "what are you waiting for"; at that point I knew he wanted me out of the company; I didn't leave, but did report him to the Director of Human Resources for unprofessional behaviour. What was really disturbing though was the change that took place in me. The bitterness and resentment, and before I knew it, my actions followed. I mean why bother to care and support other people if that's the way I'm treated? It took a dear friend of mine in the next office to have a heart to heart chat with me to show me the error of my ways.

I managed to deal with it in the end but it wasn't easy. However, as always to make it easier for you guys I've outlined some practical suggestions which not only helped me, but I can honestly say changed my life for the better. We all need to ask the question; "what kind of person do I really want to be?" When you know what kind of person you want to be, then it is easy to notice changes and deal with them at an early stage. In the end everything worked out well; I actually got out of the situation and set up my own business.

Although we don't know exactly what happened in Gehazi's case; I think it's true to say that he lost sight of his vision and sense of destiny for what God was going to do in his life. As we will see later, he ended up taking things into his own hands, literally. I've assumed that Gehazi started off well enough, but let's now consider what happened over a period of time. Gehazi is only mentioned on three separate occasions in the Bible, and we are now going to take a look at each one in turn.

4.   The Shunammite Woman

2Kings 4: v8 to 11: Elisha passed through a place called Shunem, there was a woman (referred to as a great woman) who persuaded him to stop, rest and eat before continuing on his journey. She said to her husband, "because I know Elisha is a man of God who continually passes by our house, let us set aside a room for him and provide a bed, table and chair, and some lighting so that when he arrives again we may allow him to stay with us". Sure enough, Elisha passed by and was welcomed to stay and rest.

Wow! What a woman! It's not very often that someone in the Bible is referred to as "great", but she was. Her name is not mentioned, and apart from her husband; no one else knew of her act of kindness, except obviously Elisha, but more importantly God Himself. She was certainly well to do and if I am allowed to say so, had a say in the household; that is they were a husband and wife working alongside each other in love and mutual respect.

When we think of great, we think of huge accomplishments and achievements, not normally a small act of kindness. Let me tell you about a friend of mine. A lovely young woman, her name is Marlene. One day she was walking in downtown Montreal on her way to school when she came across a lady living on the street begging for money.

What Marlene did was to go into her own bag, take out what was going to be her lunch and gave it to the woman. This lady living on the street with no home to call her own took the food, said thank you and just cried. I wonder how many times we miss out on doing an act of kindness, no matter how small, even just talking to someone - a few kind words can make all the difference.

In my book, and I mean this one, Marlene is a great (and lovely) person.

Now before I start to cry let's get back to the story:

2Kings 4: v12 to 13: Elisha asked his servant Gehazi to call the Shunammite woman and she came and stood before them. Elisha, thankful for her kindness, asked if there was anything they could do to return the favour. Since Elisha was a man of influence with the King and military commanders alike, she could have asked for anything and it would have been done for her. Instead, she said "I appreciate your offer, but we have a lovely home, and we eat well, I don't really need anything, but thanks for asking."

Yep! She was rich alright and lived well, better than most people; but that would not have stopped most people asking for more. She was content with what she had, and her lot in life, and that's a great place to be; but more on that later.

2Kings 4: v14 to 17: Elisha asks the question: what can be done for her? To which Gehazi answered by making the observation that she has no children and that her husband is old. So Gehazi called the Shunammite woman and she came and again stood before them. Elisha said to her "that by this time next year she would be holding her son." At which point she said "oh! Please don't get my hopes up too high, I've always wanted my own child but could not have one." However, what Elisha said came to pass and the Shunammite woman conceived and gave birth to a son.

Imagine how she must have felt during this time, I also think of her husband who hardly gets a mention at all. What that says to me is that although we are content with what we have, God knows our heart and innermost desires and is more than able to fulfill them. There is a passage in the Bible that not many people preach on (it's a pity really) **1 Timothy 6:v17:** which says: Don't trust in your wealth which rots way before your very eyes; but put your trust in God who provides us with everything for our enjoyment. I just want to focus on the word enjoyment; and yes God does want us to enjoy life!

2Kings 4: v18 to 37: When the child had grown, one day he went out to his father who was with the reaper, when suddenly he shouted "my head my head." The father immediately told one of the servants to carry him to his mother. The boy lay on her lap until noon and then he died. She then placed the body on the bed of the Man of God (Elisha), shut the door and went out.

She called out to her husband asking for a donkey and one of the servants, in order to go and see Elisha and quickly return back, and told her husband that everything was good. As she approached, Elisha sent Gehazi to find out if everything was all OK with her and the family, to which she replied, "everything was fine." However, when she met Elisha she took hold of his feet, at which point Gehazi came over to push her away. "Leave her alone," Elisha said, as he could see that she was really distressed but did not know why.

The Shunammite woman then shared her heart and told him "I didn't ask for a son, so why raise my hopes." Elisha then told Gehazi to take his (Elisha's) staff, run don't stop for anyone, and put it on the boy's face, while Elisha and the Shunammite woman followed. Gehazi got to the house and put the staff on the boy's face and nothing happened, so Gehazi went back to tell him that the boy had not been restored. Elisha then went into the room to see the boy dead on the bed, shut the door on both the mother and Gehazi and prayed to the LORD. To cut a long story short the boy was restored to life, given back to his mother, she bowed down, took her son and went out.

We are now going to take a look at what was going through each of their minds, an impossible task I know but bear with me. First of all the father, he is in the field with the reapers, his son then joins them, and then at some point shouts out "my head, my head"! First reaction is to get the boy back home to mum who will be able to deal with what's wrong. The father was probably unaware just how serious the situation was. The Shunammite woman (mum), she was suffering big time; all she could do was to hold her only child until he died in her arms. She must have been wondering why Elisha would give her a false hope; after all she didn't ask for anything and was content with what she had. She was hurting alright, but in all of this she did not turn her back on God, otherwise why would she immediately go to see Elisha.

What was going through Elisha's mind? Well, first of all he was surprised; prophets are still human you know; the LORD hid what was wrong, but in the end he could see her distress. I think the reason why, was that the LORD wanted Elisha to hear it directly from her. He not only heard the message but felt the emotion, I'm sure Elisha was very compassionate towards her after what she shared.

Last but not least there's Gehazi. First of all, he misread the situation and tried to push her away from Elisha. If only he had considered her acts of kindness demonstrated earlier he would have known she wasn't showing disrespect. Elisha then gives him his staff and tells him to run and place it on the boy's face. Gehazi would have run really thinking that the boy would be restored once staff was placed on his face; he was genuinely surprised and disappointed when it didn't happen; after all it was Elisha's staff, it's meant to work right? Afterwards when the boy was brought back to life, Gehazi was probably thinking "why I couldn't be in the room with Elisha, and why is it always him that does miracles?"

All well that ends well I suppose, but that wasn't the case for Gehazi as we will see in the next chapter. The Shunammite woman, we don't even know her name, but you got to love people like her.

5. Naaman: Leader of the Syrian Army

2Kings 5: v1 to 27: Naaman was a leader in the army of the king of Syria. He was held in high honour because the LORD was with him, and he was a mighty man of valour, but he had leprosy. One of the captives from the land of Israel a young girl and servant of Naaman's wife told her about a prophet in Samaria that could cure her husband's leprosy. The king of Syria gave Naaman his blessing and a letter of introduction to the king of Israel. So Naaman departed with silver, gold, and the best in clothes money can buy.

Naaman took the letter to the king of Israel, and it said he had sent his servant Naaman so that he can be cured of his leprosy. I mean the King of Israel was no doctor and he certainly wasn't God, and was suspicious thinking that the king of Syria wanted to pick a quarrel with him. At this the king got down on his knees and prayed to God; when Elisha heard this he said to the king, send him over to my place and he will know that there is a prophet in Israel. The king of Israel gave directions on how to get to Elisha's house, and Naaman turned up at the door with his horses and chariot filled with goodies. Elisha simply sent a messenger out to him saying, "go and wash in the River Jordan seven times and your leprosy will be gone."

Naaman was really disappointed, for he expected the LORD to strike the illness dead in its tracks or something like that, and to be treated with respect to which he was accustomed. He became angry and complained saying that the rivers of Damascus were far better than anything in Israel. But one of his servants persuaded him to do as the prophet said, and when he did the leprosy disappeared. Naaman and his company returned to Elisha and declared that there is no other God in all the earth except the LORD, and offered to give Elisha some of the goodies he had brought, and even though he was urged to, Elisha still refused. Naaman then promised that he would offer up sacrifices to no other gods except the LORD. Elisha said you may go in peace and so Naaman departed.

Meanwhile, Gehazi was watching all of this thinking I don't believe it; letting him get away without giving us anything. So Gehazi ran after Naaman and lied saying that his master sent him to get some silver and two changes of clothes. Naaman gave him more than he asked for and a couple of servants to carry it for him until they came close to the house. Gehazi goes into the house, and Elisha asks him, "where have you been, what have you been doing." Gehazi answered, "oh you know this and that!" To Gehazi's surprise Elisha actually did know and said, "therefore the leprosy that Naaman had will now come upon you," and Gehazi left Elisha's presence as a leper.

Gehazi started off all right, but all too quickly got disillusioned. His focus was more on Elisha rather than God; that became obvious when he moved to push away the Shunammite woman from Elisha's feet. More than that, he had a poor view of himself. He would desperately try to do something good, but to no avail. Imagine when he had Elisha's staff and placed it on the boy's face and nothing happened. If you look back to the previous chapter Gehazi expected the boy to wake up, and then, to top it all, Elisha refused payment for healing Naaman! First of all, his respect for Elisha must have gone out of the window and second, he said to himself "what about me, well if he won't accept anything, I surely will." As you can see it wasn't greed that brought him to that decision, so much as his poor self-esteem; he just wanted to be acknowledged and to feel good about himself. If it was just greed he would have gone for the gold not the silver!

Taking it to the twenty-first century; isn't it true that if someone feels down and has a lack of self-esteem, they might buy something for themselves as a little treat, or in my case a big treat. I've done it many times, and then afterwards I think, why did I get that? Don't laugh, but I tended to buy cuddle toys for myself (now I get them as presents). I remember getting a kangaroo once, didn't know what to do with it, ended up giving it away to an orphanage; well at least it went to a good home. OK make me feel good and say that I'm not the only person who does did this. Yep! That was something I used to do until I realized what was going on inside myself; more about that in the final chapter.

Gehazi had Elisha on a pedestal, and didn't look towards God. Perhaps we should ask ourselves, who do we have on a pedestal?

6.   Gehazi with the King of Israel

2Kings 8: v1 to 6: Sometime later Elisha spoke to the woman who's son he had restored to life, telling her to move because the LORD is going to bring a famine on this land for seven years. The woman left with the whole of her household and moved to the land of the Philistines until the famine was over. The Shunammite woman then returned, and made a plea to the king of Israel to get her house and land back.

Meanwhile the king of Israel was talking to Gehazi wanting to know all the great things Elisha had done. As Gehazi was telling the king about how Elisha restored a dead body to life, the Shunammite woman walked in and was making her case before the king. Gehazi said "she is the woman and this is her son who Elisha restored to life." The king heard the woman's case and appointed one of his officers to ensure that everything was restored.

Now this does end well for Gehazi. We don't know if his leprosy got healed, but we do know that he is in the presence of the king who is interested on hearing what he has to say about Elisha. Gehazi is very positive when he talked about Elisha and how the LORD used him, and I would like to believe that his self-esteem was finally restored, and everyone lived happily ever after.

Not many people end up being in the company of royalty, quite a privilege.

Time to recap: Gehazi started off well enough by providing Elisha with some insightful information regarding the Shunammite woman and the fact that she had no children. As time went on, he got more and more disillusioned and discouraged and this affected him inside. He lost sight of his self-worth. Such a person is more likely to put other people down in order to elevate themselves; note Gehazi's response to the woman when she fell at Elisha's feet. I'm sure I'm not the only one who has come across people like that.

On the other hand the Shunammite woman had every reason to have low self-esteem; she had no children which in those days was a big deal, people in the community would make fun of her. The Bible (and therefore God) referred to her - although we do not know her name - as a great woman. My point is that she had learnt to be happy and content with what she had and therefore wouldn't even think about herself so much as other people.

I'm sure not being able to have a child was always in the back of her mind, but she was strong enough to keep it there. Her big test came when Elisha said that she would give birth to a child, you can imagine after all those years, the emotions flooding back and the first thing that came to her mind was that it was a false hope; she said to Elisha: "do not lie to me to get my hopes up."

God knows the desires in the back our minds and deep in our hearts that seem impossible; so long as we are like this woman demonstrating acts of kindness and being content with what we have, (And! Are not holding onto naughty desires) don't be too surprised if God does something about it. ☺

I wish more people were like her.

7.   Confessions of a Chronic Complainer

OK! We are well and truly back in the twenty first century, and we are talking about me here, so what can be done? Remember me at work (Chapter 3), low self-esteem, the what-about-me syndrome which in the end would have destroyed me were it not for a dear friend; who got me thinking: what kind of person do I really want to be? But first of all I had to take a long look in the mirror in order to see who I had become.   Hence   I've   called   this   chapter "Confessions of a Chronic Complainer", chronic because it was long term and in the background, hardly noticeable, unlike the acute form which can be heard from the other side of the company cafeteria.

"Don't complain and talk about your problems; 80% of people don't care; the other 20% will think you deserve them."~Mark Twain

There is a link between this and self-esteem. If you feel hard done by or not fairly treated, disillusioned, or feel discontent; all of these things will put you down over a period of time. Sometimes, people will deliberately try to destroy your self-esteem for their own ends.   Yep! That's happened to me alright. Here is where you have to make some tough choices, am I going to stay the way I am, or am I going to change? The key is rebuilding your self-esteem, and feel good about yourself again, and the rest will follow.

What worked well for me was to first of all start to be thankful and develop a thankful attitude. It wasn't easy at first, but then everything started to fit into place. We all have something to be thankful for no matter how small and that's the starting point. I also had to be content with my "lot in life", in other words to be content and happy with what I already have instead of complaining of what I don't have.

Let's face it; if we are always complaining at what we don't have, we actually lose enjoying what we do have. We live in a society today where everyone wants more, we are never satisfied. A bigger house, a higher paying job, a better, newer car, and these lists go on. That was exactly what was happening to me, I was effectively destroying myself from the inside. When I started to see what I actually had and gave thanks, I started to have a better view of myself, and started to take an interest in other people and how to encourage them. Show me a person who has good self-esteem and I will show you a person who is humble and takes an interest in other people instead of focusing on themselves.

Also, remember what happened when I was younger (Chapter 2); my parents did not do everything for me, but gave me the support and resources to be successful leading to my good self-esteem, and being rewarded for my efforts was all part and parcel of it. As parents, we can actually give too much to our children and effectively destroy their self-esteem. Let me put it another way; we give our children the latest technology, computers, cell phones, and everything else. I can almost guarantee that the activities that they would undertake would include social media, computer games, getting into the latest fashions; none of these so called activities are great at truly building up one's self-esteem or worth, because nothing has really been achieved.

Take for example, winning at computer games: when you really think about it, it's a false sense of achievement. It's not as if you are flying an aeroplane, or snowboarding down a slope. With social media, true we learn a lot of facts, but all that crap too; all that advertising; making people feel inadequate unless they get the latest and the best money can buy. I can see that's doing wonders for your self-esteem, and do people really know how to interact with each other, or are we becoming so dependent on computer dating.

Honestly, what has happened to the days when a child would take up music, a team sport, or a hobby and actually do something, and if you can get paid for it all the better, now that builds up one's self-esteem. So, for all you parents out there; don't allow your children to laze about over their computers, get them to help out working alongside you, and encourage more suitable activities; it will really build them up.

"Great people talk about ideas; Average people talk about things; Small people talk about other

people; and then sadly there are people who just love to talk about themselves"...... Oops! I did a bit.

Cultivating a thankful heart will transform your life as it did with me. But I believe it will only be the case when you know Jesus Christ as your personal LORD & Savior that you will be truly happy and fulfilled. God can do it and enable you to be thankful in all of your circumstances.

I never thought about this before, but it occurred to me that we have comparative examples of two people. First of all Gehazi, who had everything going for him as the assistant of the greatest and most influential prophet of his day, and then there was the Shunammite woman who had every reason to have low self-esteem because she didn't have children, which was a big deal culturally in those days. Out of these two people, when it comes to self-esteem, it was the Shunammite woman not Gehazi who won through in the end. She was the one God referred to as "great", not only because of her acts of kindness, but also the fact that she was content with her lot in life, which was not the case with Gehazi.

Perhaps the title of this book should really be:

Everything I Know About Self-esteem I Got From The Shunammite Woman

While I was writing this book I was thinking that I would like to be more like the Shunammite woman just to do some acts of kindness. I think if more of us did, the world would be a better place ☺